That's So Orff!

Lessons, Songs, and Activities for the Elementary Classroom

Jennifer Kamradt

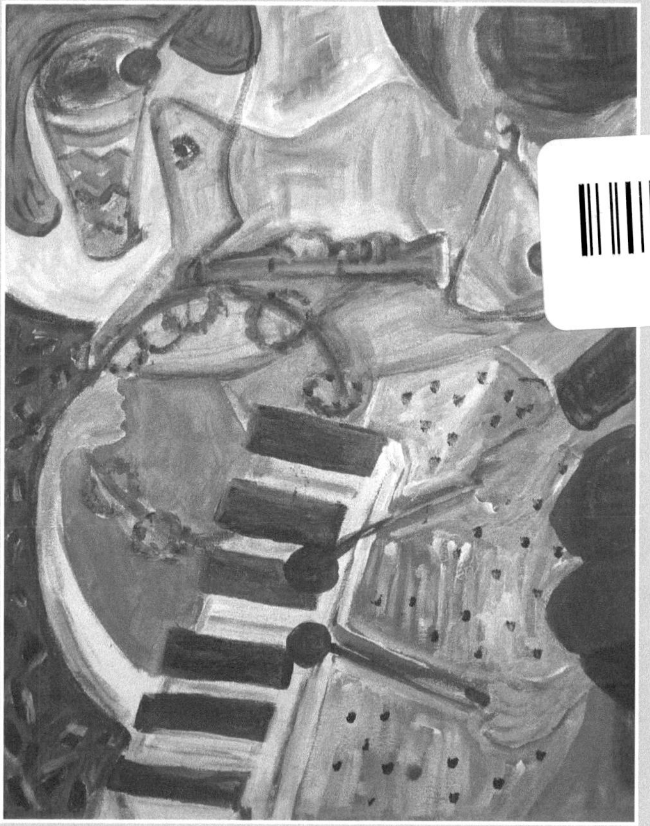

Alfred

alfred.com

ISBN-10: 1-4706-1037-X
ISBN-13: 978-1-4706-1037-1

Cover Art:
Orff Instruments by Rosemary Grant

ONLINE ACCESS INCLUDED

Download the PDF content for this book.
To access online media, visit: **alfred.com/redeem**
Enter the following code:

0042360-12859344

Table of Contents

About the Author

Jennifer Kamradt is a music teacher at West Lincoln-Broadwell Elementary School in Lincoln, IL. She received a Bachelor's degree from Illinois State University and a Master's degree from the University of Illinois. Jennifer has received all three levels of Orff-Schulwerk training at Illinois State University and has presented at the Illinois State Music Educators conferences and the American Orff-Schulwerk Association conference.

Acknowledgments

To Steve and Cathy, whose support has made this book a reality.
To all my students at West Lincoln-Broadwell through the years—you have helped make these pieces and myself a success.

Notes for this Book

- Orff is a process that does not need the use of "Orff" instruments to be successful. The parts presented in this book may be adapted in any manner.

- The use of objects/props adds an additional visual flare to any program. Programs in which these are incorporated hold real audience appeal and only increase advocacy for the music program.

- We can truly see the gifts and talents of our students when we reach for high expectations. On a side note: I never really knew that many of my students held hidden talents until I handed them a swirly hoop.

Instrumentation Key

SG	Soprano Glockenspiel
AG	Alto Glockenspiel
SM	Soprano Metallophone
AM	Alto Metallophone
BM	Bass Metallophone
BX	Bass Xylophone
SX	Soprano Xylophone
AX	Alto Xylophone
CB	Contra Bass Bars

BI	All Barred Instruments
Xylo.	All Xylophone Instruments
FC	Finger Cymbals
WC	Wind Chimes
HD	Hand Drum
Cym.	Suspended Cymbal
Tom	Roto-Tom
SH	Swirly Hoop
Tr.	Triangle

A Brighter Place

Grade Level: Kindergarten

Concepts: Beat, Rhythm, Structured Instrumental Improvisation, and Free Movement Improvisation

Materials: Any set of Orff Instruments, Streamers, Ribbons, Scarves, and Ring Scarves

Process

Prior to Lesson

- Establish the concept of beat in the classroom with various teaching strategies and activities.
- Establish the difference between **beat** and **rhythm**.

Beat

- Introduce the beat played on the xylophone. The piece is used as an introduction to the barred instruments. If there are too many coordination issues, playing only the C will work, as well.
- Play the drum, and ask the students to play along.
- Make a game out of the beat. Pick a number, but do not reveal it to the students. Have the students listen and try to determine the number. This develops the students' listening skills and the ability to stop together as a group.
- Sing the song on "la," while students play the beat. Have the students join singing when they are comfortable.
- Teach the song by rote. Continue having students play the beat on bass xylophone until they are able to play by themselves.
- While singing, add the soprano glockenspiel/alto glockenspiel part by snapping during the appropriate rhythmic spot.

Rhythm

- Having set up the xylophone in C pentatonic (C D E G A), establish the rhythm of the song by speaking the lyrics.
- Have students pat the rhythm on body percussion. Note that the hand usage is one in which the hands are alternating.
- Ask students to play the rhythm of the song on the barred instruments. They may play any note they wish.
- Check that students are transferring body percussion to mallet technique.

Movement

- Establish rules for the use of props in the room.
- Have students sing the song, and use props as a beat instrument within the A section. They can:
    - Tap streamer sticks together.
    - Move in a steady beat.
    - Use ring scarves.
- Have students speak the song and use creative movement with the props within the B section.

Note: Ring scarves are the author's innovation and offer an effective, aesthetically pleasing way to tap the beat. Sew scarves onto diving rings so that students can grip the rings and let the scarves fly. These are especially great for special learners.

Combination

- Practice the transition between sections of beat and rhythm.
- Allow students to experience both movement and instrumental improvisation.
- Allow students to perform the continuous beat on the bass xylophone. The ability to continue a beat without assistance through the B section and with added rhythm playing is a great assessment tool.

Extensions

- Ask students how they can make the world a better place. Take ideas and form a speech chant as an additional section of the music.
- Add body percussion to the lyrics and transfer this exercise to non-pitched percussion.

A Brighter Place

Jennifer Kamradt

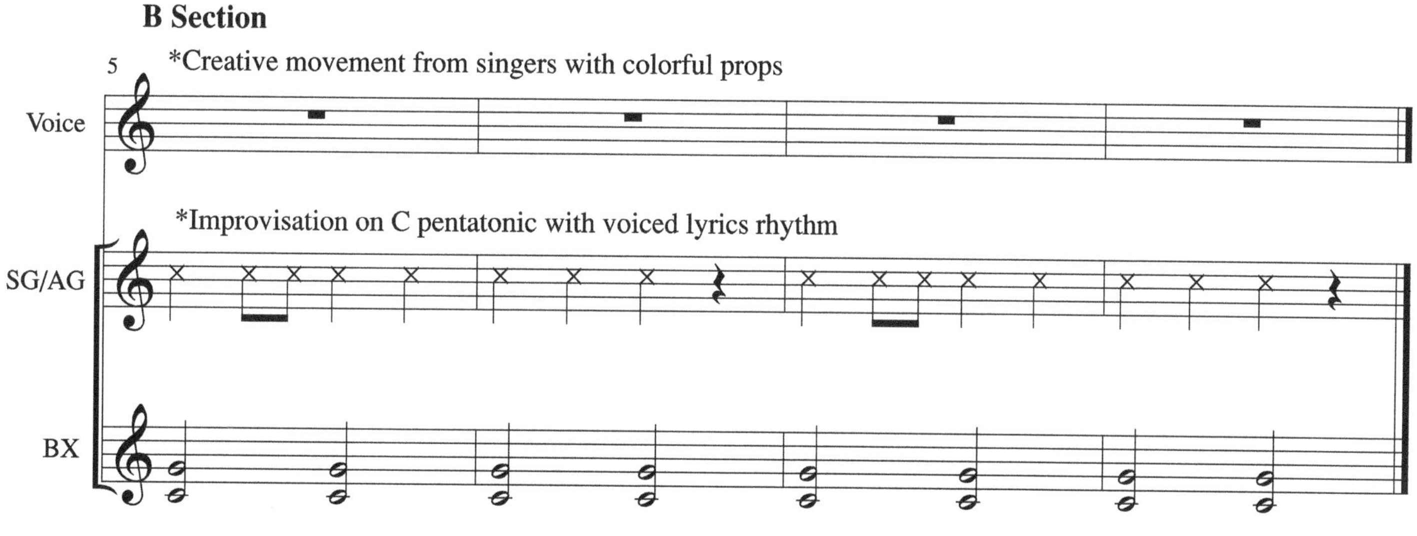

Blowing in the Wind

Grade Level: K–1

Concepts: Beat/Basic Bordun, Structured Improvisation, Improvised Movement, Coda, Form, and Melodic Direction

Materials: BX, SG/AG, and SX/AX
Scarves and Lanterns

Process

Beat and Song/A Section

- Introduce the beat by patting and singing a song on neutral syllables. It is important that the patting is done simultaneously with both hands and not alternated.
- Move the students to barred instruments. Transfer patting to all barred instruments while continuing to sing on a neutral syllable. If there are not enough instruments, adding drums will also work. This way, all students are playing.
- Teach song by rote, leaving out the spoken section and focusing on beat playing.
- To help teach melodic direction, place the lyrics on the board, after students learn the song. Write out the lyrics in phrases. It may be helpful to use shapes to mark the form. For example: ■ ● ■ ★
- Using the melodic shapes, write the words out, and draw the shapes under the notes.

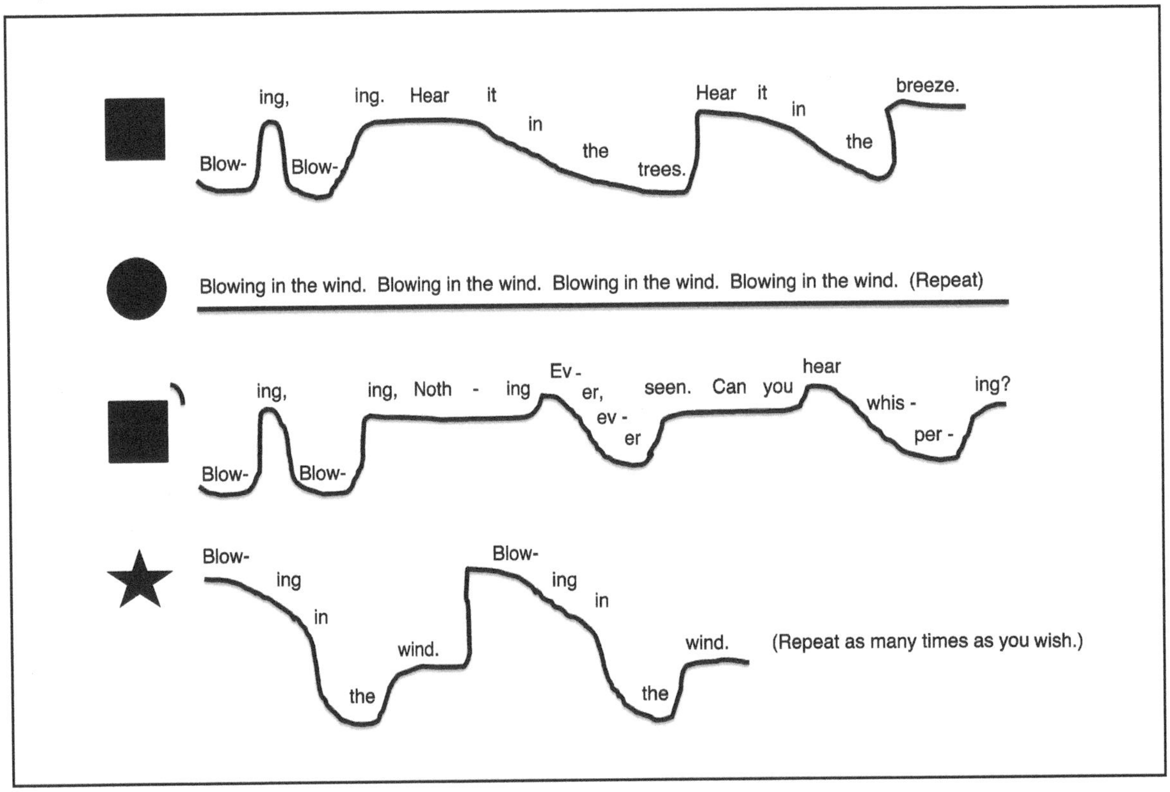

- Discuss the similarities and differences in melodic direction among sections.
- Practice until students are comfortable.

Glissando/A Section and Coda

- Introduce the glissando on the glockenspiels.
- Work on a slower glissando instead of an incredibly fast glissando.
- Teach only the glissando that occurs on the word "blowing." After students are comfortable, add the other glissandi.

Note: When teaching this part of the song, it is helpful to use a visual reference for the words, like an upward arrow under all the instances of "blowing."

Structured Improvisation/B Section

- Introduce the spoken ostinato. Practice using the rest effectively during this exercise.
- Add body percussion by patting both legs. It is important that patting is done with alternating hands and not simultaneously.
- Transfer the body percussion to the instruments. Students may play whatever notes they wish, as long as they are playing the correct rhythm.
- Practice going between the spoken/played sections of the song.
- Introduce the Coda. Repeat any number of times. Adding dynamics such as diminuendos creates another effect and teaches students to play musically.

Movement

- Introduce the concept of trees and blowing wind.
- Have students stand in place during the singing sections and move freely during the improvised-melody section.
- Give students scarves for a more visual effect. Using lanterns can add a "firefly" effect and can be very cool in a darkened performance space, especially by draping the scarves on top of the lanterns.
- To maintain a little more control with the movement, have the students "rooted" to their spots, like trees, and only move the upper body. Or have some students remain stationary while "Lantern" students make pathways through space.

Note: Lanterns can be found at any bargain store and are effective because students can use their handles to maintain a good grip. Using other objects like flashlights or battery-operated candles would be effective as well.

Useful Tips

- Designate certain instruments for glissandi only and improvisation only to simplify bar set-up. This might be easier with students who need simpler parts and, consequently, can focus on playing just one part. However, with more advanced classes, students can play both the glissandi and rhythmic improvisation on their instruments.
- The use of visual aids is especially helpful for reinforcing the vocal line.

Blowing in the Wind

Jennifer Kamradt

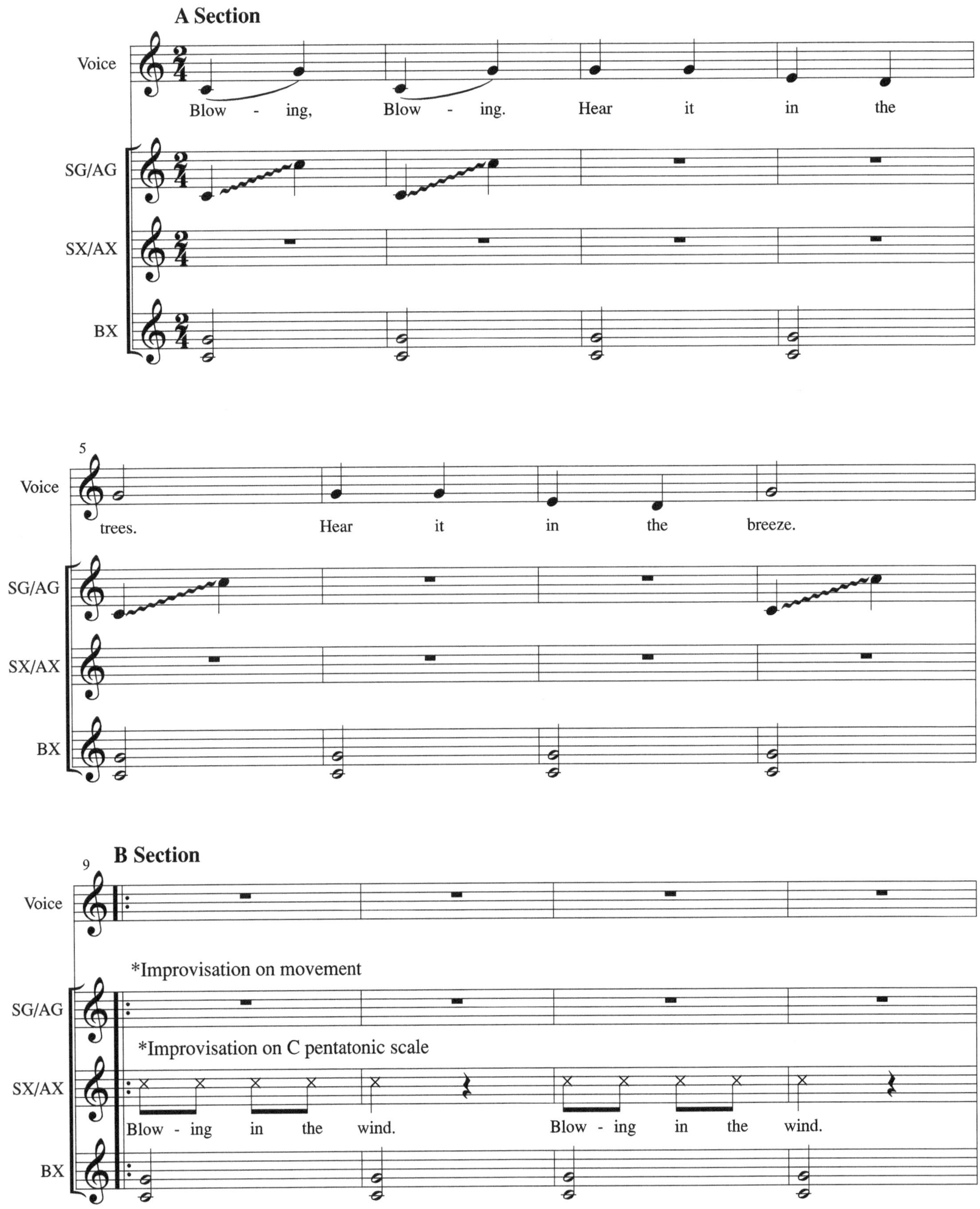

13
Voice
SG/AG
SX/AX
Blow - ing in the wind. Blow - ing in the wind.
BX
17
A¹ Section
Voice
Blow - ing, Blow - ing. Noth - ing ev - er, ev - er
SG/AG
SX/AX
BX
21
Voice
seen. Can you hear the whis - per - ing?
SG/AG
SX/AX
BX
25
Coda
Voice
Blow - ing in the wind. Blow - ing in the wind.
SG/AG
SX/AX
BX

Your Crown

Grade Level: K–1

Concepts: Beat, Rhythm, $\frac{6}{8}$, Form, and Structured Improvisation

Materials: SG/AG, SX/AX, AM, BX, HD, and FC

Process

Beat

- Introduce many activities with beat. Instead of passing a beat, work on individual control of the beat. The transfer to the instruments will be quicker if students practice individually rather than waiting to receive their turns at passing the beat.

Examples of beat activities:

- Even though the students are young, giving students individual balls to bounce on the beat is a great activity. Having the students sit on the floor instead of standing helps with ball control, as do rules for what happens when balls are lost.
- Using music and patting the beat on different parts of the body keeps everyone actively involved.

Useful Tips

- Bounce a tennis ball on the Tubano drum to amplify the sound and to be heard above all the other bouncing balls.
- When students have become adept, transfer the beat to the barred instruments and hand drums, while continuing to play the beat with a drum.
- Use a mallet on the Tubano drum to increase the volume of the sound, so it is heard over all the instruments.
- Add the soprano glockenspiel/alto glockenspiel and finger cymbal lines by the transfer of body percussion to the instruments. Work on the beat with the soprano glockenspiel/alto glockenspiel part by having students play eight beats and adding a "ding" on beats 4 and 8.

Song/A Section

- While playing the beat on bass xylophone and drums, sing the song multiple times.
- Teach the song by rote.
- Students should sing and play until they are comfortable.
- When students have become adept at playing the beat by themselves, transition into the "heartbeat" rhythm for drum players.

Improvisation/B Section

- Continue practicing the beat together while playing the song rhythmically on a barred instrument.
- Teach the students that the line is played exactly how it would be sung. Mentally speaking the song will help the transfer.
- Students can improvise on any D pentatonic scale (D E F A B).
- Work on a fluid transfer between sections.

Coda

- Discuss what a **coda** is in musical terms.
- Introduce the use of the repeat, and sing "Your Crown" four times.
- Teach how to end the song.
- Practice the entire song until students are comfortable.

Useful Tips

- When teaching this song, it helps to have visual references for the form of the song. For example:

  ■ Beat with "ding" on 4 and 8

  ● Beat with song

  ★ Rhythmically improvised song
  Repeat as many time as necessary before going to the Coda.

  ▲ "Coda" beat with "crown" four times

  ■ Beat with "ding" on 4 and 8 (Group adds a "ding" on the downbeat or beat 9.)

Extensions

- If the piece is too challenging for some classes, the drum line can simply play the beat.

At a Program

- "Your Crown" is about an imaginary crown that every child has. Ask each child what his or her crown would look like, and add a section to be spoken individually.
- To connect the material presented to the visual arts, work with the art teacher. This can include creating paintings of each child with the crown on his or her head.
- Through the use of music, children's voices, art, and a baby picture from home, this turns into an emotional, heart-warming piece for any program, guaranteed to have families going home with tears in their eyes.

  Form for the song in a program:

  - ❖ Introduction/Song and Slide Show of a Few Students' Artwork
  - ❖ Improvised Section Repeat with Slide Show of Baby Pictures and Students' Recorded Voices describing their crowns
  - ❖ Continue until all pictures have been seen.
  - ❖ Crown Ending and Coda

Your Crown

Jennifer Kamradt

B Section
18
Voice
Look at the col-ors that shine.
Improvisation on any of the following notes: D E F A B
SG/AG
FC
Xylo.
HD
Coda
24
Your crown!
Your crown!
30

Oh, No!

Grade Level: 2–3

Concepts: Pitch Development, Minor Tonality, Repeat, Melodic Direction, and Stepwise Motion vs. Leap

Materials: SG/AG, SX/AX, SM/AM, BX, and FC or Tr.

Process

Part 1 Instrumental

- Using both upwards and downwards motives, echo sing on neutral syllables in the key of D minor.

Note: If students have trouble with stepwise motion versus leaps, using visual references or hand signs can be beneficial. It also serves as a reference point.

- Have students choose instruments. (Set them up in D minor: D E F A B♭.) Sing the pattern, and ask students to find it on their instruments. The patterns will be those of the soprano glockenspiel/alto glockenspiel line. This will help students develop their auditory listening skills. If they are having trouble, move over and sing with them until they find the starting notes.

Note: If there are not enough barred instruments for all students, have them work in pairs.

- Add a visual notational reference once the notes are learned. The students will begin to piece together what they hear and see.
- Practice the soprano glockenspiel/alto glockenspiel line until students are comfortable.
- Add a bass xylophone part using speech: "Oh, this is bad."
- Add a finger cymbal part. Substituting high-pitched percussion works as well.

Note: Adding a two-bar bass xylophone introduction helps return to the beginning after a repeat.

Part 2 Song with Instrumental

- Set xylophones up in D minor pentatonic.
- Sing the vocal line and use body percussion to teach the xylophone part.

Note: The hardest section in the xylophone part is playing through the sung word "shall." All the other syllables are echoed from the vocal line.

- Students should practice body percussion parts before transferring them to the xylophones. The students can play any note, as long as they play the accurate rhythm.
- Add the bass xylophone part on the words "No-No-Shall-Do."
- Teach the song by rote, if it hasn't already been learned through listening.
- Repeat and work on the transitions between the two parts of the song.

Coda

- Sing the vocal line of the Coda, and have students echo.
- Since instruments should already be set up in D minor pentatonic, have the students "walk" down the scale and end with the earlier bass xylophone part: "Oh, this is bad."

Extensions

- You can repeat the song as many times as needed and add in B sections.
    - Ask students for reasons why they may be singing, "Oh, no!"
    - Ask students for solutions to any "Oh, no!" mistakes.
    - Ask students to develop a dramatic scene during the Part 1 instrumental section.
    - This piece can be used in conjunction with a story line that plays out multiple times.
      For example:
      A section—Song and "Oh, No!" problem
      B section—Student-created rhythmic solution

Oh, No!

Jennifer Kamradt

9
Part 2
Voice
no! Oh, no! What shall we do? Oh, no! Oh, no! What
SG/AG
*Xylophones improvise on the following notes: D E F A B♭
SX/AX
FC
BX
13
shall we do? Wait! I think we got it!
17
Yes we did!

Baker's Song

Grade Level: 2–3

Concepts: Ostinato, Student Created Rhythms, Form, and Rhythm Identification

Materials: SG/AG, SX/AX, SM/AM, BX, Tom, and HD or Tubanos
Kitchen Materials: Bowls, Wooden Spoons, Pots, Silverware, Spices/Sprinkles, etc.

Process

Student-Created Speech

- Create a word bank of bakery-themed items.
- Make word cards and put them on the white board, or create something using a SmartBoard or PowerPoint.
- Put up rhythmic units of one- or two-beat durations.
- Have students move the word cards into the appropriate rhythmic unit.
- Have students try all forms of the rhythmic unit with the words to see which sounds the best.
- Break up into groups, and ask each group to pick six to eight words from different rhythmic units. This works best when the majority of the rhythms are in different categories, but a few in the same one will work as well.
- Groups can then practice arranging the words into a rhythmic sentence. It is important to not always go with the first choice but to rearrange several times.
- Ask students to decide which words to use in the group, based on where rhythms sound the best.

Note: It is important to lead the students to the desirable answer, but if they have a strong feeling that a word should be somewhere, let them use their desired outcome.

- Depending on the desired outcome, here are a few ideas:
    - Add body percussion to the speech.
    - Add body percussion, and practice internalizing the speech.
    - Add different colored instruments to different groups or within groups, i.e. woods, metals, shakers-scrapers, and drums.
    - Or to make it more interesting, add kitchen items. This section can also be layered in as the students come on or off the stage before Verse 1.
- Here is an example of an effective form:
    - Introduction
    - Verse 1
    - Group 1 Speech/Stomping

- Verse 2
- Group 1 (one time through), add Group 2 Speech/Snapping
- Verse 3
- Group 1 add Group 2 add Group 3 Speech/Patting
- Verse 4
- Group 1 add Group 2 add Group 3 add Group 4 Speech/Clapping
- Group 1 add Group 2 add Group 3 add Group 4 Body Percussion Only
- Group 1 add Group 2 add Group 3 add Group 4 Instruments/Kitchen Items

Accompaniment

- Teach the rhythm, "Cup-Cake-Coo-kies-Pies-and-Tarts," without using speech. Have students listen to the rhythm played on the drum and recreate the rhythm on the board.
- Add speech to reinforce the rhythm. Practice saying and using body percussion with the rhythm.
- Have students play the rhythm on hand drums. Transfer a few students to the soprano glockespiel/alto glockenspiel and soprano xylophone/alto xylophone parts. This part is exactly like the drum part, but split between instruments.
- Play the beat on bass xylophone, soprano metallophone/alto metallophone, and roto-tom. Practice with a two-bar intro, and establish the speech rhythm before layering in barred instruments.

Song

- The song can be taught by rote or with neutral syllables.
- By adding the accompaniment and singing the parts to students, they have more opportunities to hear the song before singing it themselves.
- Practice the whole song together.

Extensions

- Kitchen items that work well:
    - Plastic bowls and wooden spoons
    - Shakers—Containers filled with beans
    - Metal sounds—Large cafeteria serving spoons
- Have some fun and dress the baking part!

Baker's Song

Jennifer Kamradt

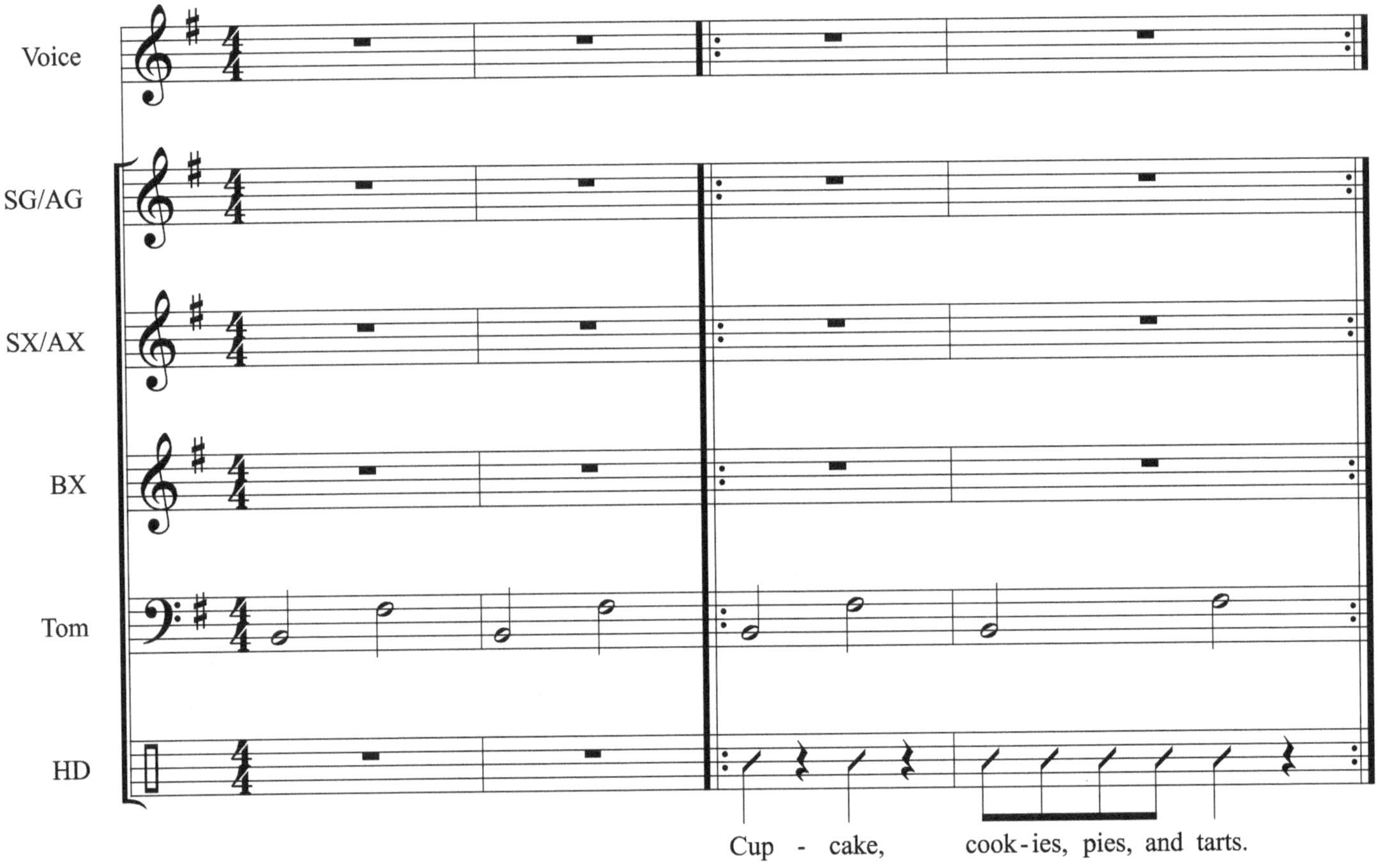

5
1. Bak - er, bak - er, bak - ing treats. Bak - ing, bak - ing some-thing sweet.
2. Yum - my, yum - my, tastes so great! Is there more? I can - not wait.
3. Sprin-kles, ic - ing on the top. Give me more, please. Do not stop!
4. Bak - er, bak - er, bak - ing treats. Bak - ing, bak - ing some-thing sweet.
SG/AG
SX/AX
BX
Tom
HD

9
*Insert baking rhythms created by students.
SG/AG
SX/AX
BX
Tom
HD

Swirly Hoop Song

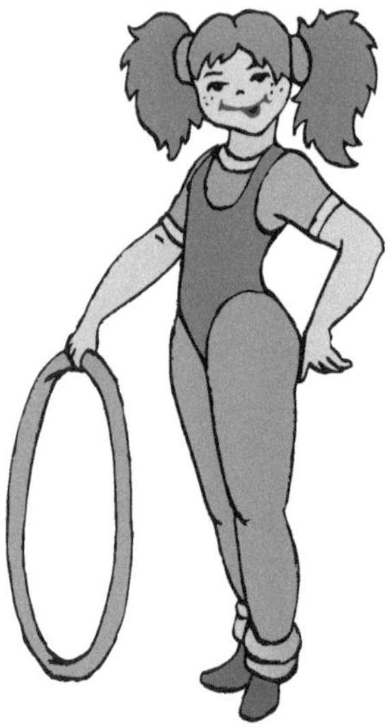

Grade Level: 2–3

Concepts: Chords, Form, and Meter of 3

Materials: BX, AG/SG, SX/AX, and SH (Swirly Hoop)

Process

Form of the Piece: ABAC

The A Section

- Introduce the meter of 3 using musical selections and individual beat development. Have students find the strong beat 1.
- Add movement with feet in 3, and continue patting or bouncing a ball on 1.
- Practice until students are comfortable.
- Introduce the bass xylophone part using body percussion. Left-Right-Cross. If an easier bass xylophone part is desired, change the part, and teach using this speech: "Yeah, swirly hoops!" Play as a bordun on C and G. Continue movement and patting as students practice the cross-over bordun.
- Teach the glockenspiel melody to the entire class using only the strong beats.
- Practice until students are comfortable, then add eighth notes to finish the melody.
- Practice both bass xylophone and soprano glockenspiel/alto glockenspiel parts together until comfortable.
- Introduce the soprano xylophone/alto xylophone part by using body percussion and speech: "This is fun! This is fun! This is fun! That's right!" When transferring to the barred instruments, transfer the rhythm and notes to C and G. After the students are comfortable, make the note change to D and A.
- Practice all parts together until comfortable.
- Add in the swirly hoop part. This part should be played by lightly tapping the hoop on the floor. (Hard floors are the best.) This turns the hoop into a rhythmic instrument.
- The A section should be played twice.

Note: The glockenspiels will play a glissando to signal the transition to the B section. There will be no transition or glissando from B to A.

The B Section

- All students should learn the melody together, starting with the rhythm. Referring back to the bass xylophone part in the A section, use the same speech, ("Yeah, swirly hoops!"), and review with body percussion.
- Take the rhythm and transfer to the instruments, but only play the note G. "Walk" down the instrument and stop on B.
- Instruct students on the chords, intervals, or space, or whichever way works best in your classroom. Add the left-hand E with the right-hand G.
- Practice moving hands down the xylophone together and keeping the spacing of the third intervals. Stop on G and B.
- Teach the students to play F–A and G–B as "walking" back up in quarter rhythms, and then play high C and low C. You can teach this through body percussion as well.
- Practice until students are comfortable.

Note: The melody is played on all glockenspiels, xylophones, and metallophones, but not on any bass instruments. This is for a lighter color contrast in the B section.

- Add the swirly hoop part. The hoop is used as a visual aspect in this section. The hoop should make "circles."

Note: This section does not involve placing the hoop on the body and twirling. The focus here is a visual element to complement the lighter instrumental arrangement.

  - Circle in front slowly.
  - Put the toy hoop on the floor, and spin.
  - Hop through the toy hoop.
  - Circle around the back and front like a butterfly.

- Play the B section twice, then return to the A section.

The C Section

- Teach the students how to play a "roll" using two mallets. Ask students to play on the lowest possible C and as fast as they can without playing harshly on the bars.
- Give a cue for finishing the section and having all students play the low C together.
- Using the speech from the A and B sections, review with body percussion: "Yeah, swirly hoops!"
- Add the final rhythm on C–G after the low C is played as a group.
- Practice rolls and the final rhythm until students are comfortable.
- Add the swirly hoop part. The hoops here will twirl in a typical rotating fashion. Have students visually be on different parts of the body.

  Example:

  - Waist
  - Arm
  - Neck
  - Knees
  - Ankles

A Few Notes

- As much as it hurts to not end on the A section, it really is necessary. The C section is so fun and crowd-pleasing that going back to A just doesn't end with the same finality. However, students should still be taught the musical concept of traditional rondo form.
- Adding non-pitched percussion is also acceptable.
  - The A section xylophone part could be played on a number of instruments.
  - The A section bass xylophone part could be played on drums.
  - The C section could be played by anything that shakes.

Swirly Hoop Song

Jennifer Kamradt

B Section

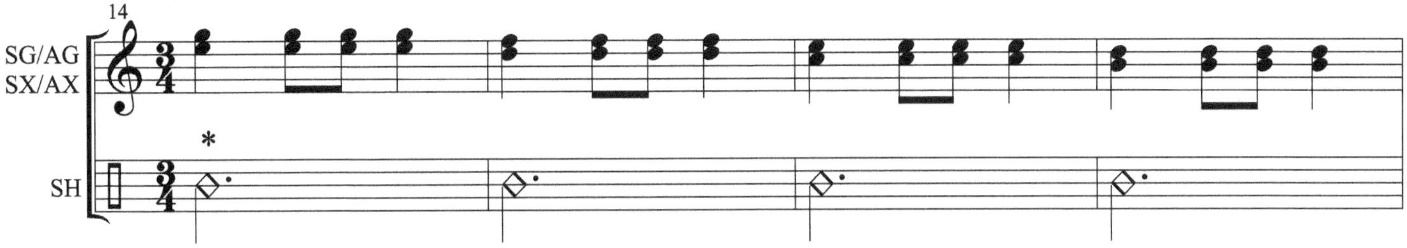

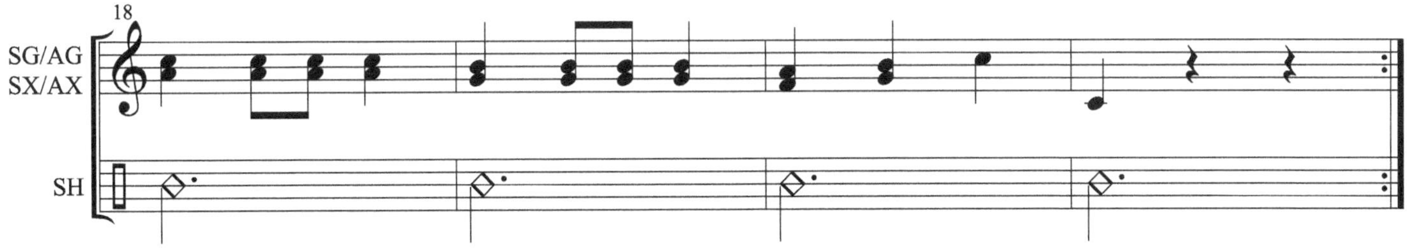

Swirly hoops are used as "visual effect." Make circles and shapes with hoops.

- Circle in front slowly.
- Put the toy hoop on the floor, and spin.
- Hop through the toy hoop.
- Circle around the back and front like a butterfly.

C Section

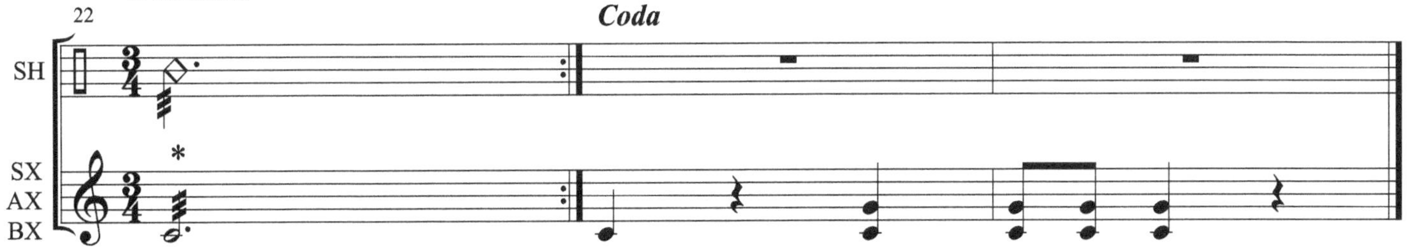

*Roll on low C as hoopers twirl in traditional fashion.
When significant time has passed, start the Coda as hoopers strike a pose.

Chocolate Fudge

Grade Level: 4–5

Concepts: Meter of $\frac{6}{8}$, Improvisation, Rhythms in $\frac{6}{8}$, Balance, and Soloist

Materials: SG/AG, SX/AX, and BX

Process

Instrumental Accompaniment

- Introduce the bass xylophone line by using body percussion and transferring to the barred instrument. Use speech, "Fudge, Fudge, Chocolate, Fudge."
- Add the soprano/alto xylophone and soprano/alto glockenspiel lines by patting or snapping body percussion. Use speech, "Chocolate, Chocolate, Chocolate, Fudge-Ding-Ding."
- Practice until students are comfortable.

Solo/Improvisation

- Set up the barred "solo" instrument in D pentatonic (D E F A B), or use soprano recorders. Have students experiment with melodic ideas.
- Discuss the rhythms commonly found in $\frac{6}{8}$, and let students experiment with those motives.
- Discuss ways to improvise.
    - Come up with a desired motive, and repeat it.
    - Pick a favorite note. For example, E–F, E–A, E–B, etc.
    - Change dynamics.
    - Play rolls on a single note or different notes.
    - Add grace notes.
    - Add passing tones.
    - Experiment with high-range melodies, low-range melodies, or traveling melodies.
    - Use single-handed, double-handed, or alternated techniques.
    - Experiment with dissonance and resolution.
    - Try stepwise motion or leaps in the melody.
    - Distinguish between playing the same motive as the group versus playing one's own rhythm.
    - Improvise with two students at the same time.
    - Perform complementary rhythms and range with another improvising student.
- Discuss balance between the barred instruments and the soloist.
- Let students explore and have many opportunities to improvise. The students should be on a rotation, moving between instruments and playing all parts.

Useful Tip

- Improvise with students. By playing with them, they develop a foundation for their own improvisation ideas.

Chocolate Fudge

Jennifer Kamradt

Community

Grade Level: 5–6

Concepts: Canon, Vocal Technique, and Harmony

Materials: Piano

Process

- Sing the song on a neutral syllable.
- Teach the song by phrases, with neutral syllables.
- Add a solfège syllable to each phrase.
- Combine phrases together—phrases 1 and 2, and then phrase 3.
- Have students practice until they are comfortable.
- Add words to the song, and help students practice until they are comfortable.
- Focus on students' pitch development. Only use the piano, if necessary, for the starting pitch.
- Break students into two groups, and have them sing the song in a two-part canon. Repeat several times, and end on a fermata.
- Break students into three groups, and have them sing the song in a three-part canon. Repeat several times, and end on a fermata.

Useful Tip

- The use of this canon is pretty effective at the beginning of the year as the classroom setting is developed. The piece was written with the intent to build the classroom as a community and encourage students to work together for success.

Community

Jennifer Kamradt

Dragon Song

Grade Level: 4–5

Concepts: Rondo Form, "La" Centered Pentatonic, Group Movement, Beat, Echo, and Dynamics

Materials: BX, SX/AX, SG/AG, HD, WC, FC, Cym./Gong, and Recorder
A homemade or purchased full-body dragon!

Process

Speech Chant

- Introduce the echo and two-part speech.
- Have students perform with varying levels of dynamics as written and while moving through space.
- Stress the importance of rests. During the rests, have students use the time to visually "look for the dragon!"
- Stress the importance of continuous movement to add to the notion of an incoming dragon.
- Have students' movement end in the space where their instruments lie, to be ready to perform the introduction without any significant break or added rests.

Introduction

- Use body percussion to demonstrate the rhythm of the Introduction. It is important to use different body percussion for both the high and low tones.
- Ask students to create the rhythm. For example: As a class, students write the rhythm on the white board or work in groups with rhythm cards to assemble the rhythm.
- Students will naturally hear the half notes as quarter notes, so try to keep the hand movement continuous during the half-note duration.
- Have students perform using body percussion until they are comfortable.
- Transfer rhythms to drums. If using hand drums, establish the proper up-and-down motion. If using Tubanos, establish the tones.
- Have the students practice until they are comfortable. Practice controlling volume, keeping the music slow and quiet. Add dynamic changes each time to build the anticipation of the dragon entrance.
- Practice the transition from speech chant to the Introduction. There will be no break between any of the sections. If using the hand drums, a visual effect can be added to the speech chant durning the rests.

A Section

- Teach the recorder part by the **skeleton method.***
- Start with strong beats and add the passing tones.
- Add the drum part with the recorder to provide the beat, especially through the dotted half notes.
- Add the bass xylophone roll.
- Add the cymbal and wind chime parts. The cymbal should be played with a yarn mallet. Strike just one crash, making sure that it is not too abrupt. The wind chime should be played from low to high with one continuous, slow ascent.
- Practice until students are comfortable, and build on to include the transitions between Speech and Introduction.

B Section

- Teach the main melody using speech. You can use the following: "Cho-co-late Coo-kie, Cho-co-late Cake. Cho-co-late Cook-ie, Yum-my Cake." The tones for the drum should all be high and played on the edge. This part can also be played by using soft mallets on the Tubano drum head. If played this way, the rhythm can be easily played faster and louder than the beat that the drums are playing. This part can also be played on temple blocks.
- Add the beat on all low tones with other drums. Have the students practice until they are comfortable.
- Add the finger cymbal, cymbal, and wind chime parts through body percussion.
- Repeat this section.
- It is important that all other drums stop and let the cymbal and wind chimes have their "moment."
- Add the A section again after the B section. Have the students practice until they are comfortable, and work on the transitions between sections.

C Section

- Teach the first melody using the skeleton method. Remember to set up in C pentatonic (C D E G A).
- Teach the Improvisation section using body percussion. The improvised melody is played on the C pentatonic scale.
- Teach the second melody using the skeleton method.
- Put all four phrases together.
- Teach the bass xylophone part with speech: "Drag-on, here it comes!" Add to the melody.
- Add the drum beat and finger cymbals.
- Practice until students are comfortable, and work on transitions between all sections.

Movement

- Teach the dragon dance with the whole class.
- Practice in one "conga" line, or break up into multiple conga lines. It makes the movement easier if each line has about six students. Stress the importance of physical space and avoiding neighbors' spaces.
- Work on movement throughout the room and not just in a circle.
- Using a bigger space is ideal for teaching this part of the piece—a gym or outside area works beautifully!

Some Notes

- The form of this piece is ABACA.
- Creating a dragon is a wonderful addition to this piece.

*The **skeleton method** is best used when adding a visual reference. Create a visual aid, and block out the note(s) not being taught. Remove the blocked visuals (by using PowerPoint, SmartBoard, etc.), and restore them when there has been significant practice.

Tips for Dragon Making

- Get a long piece of fabric, or piece together different fabrics. Check the remnant or discount bin at a fabric store, or ask people who sew.
- Sew the fabric together.
- Ask parents to sew on the scales. Use the template included or one of your own.
- For the dragon head, use Styrofoam. First draw the dragon head on the material, then cut out two pieces. These will be two sides of the head. Score cardboard by turning it over and using scissors to cut grooves into it, making it pliable. Use hot glue with cardboard to connect the two Styrofoam head pieces. For the harder-to-form parts of the dragon, try foam pieces from a local fabric store.
- Paint as desired. Attach the fabric body to the dragon head, or have the two pieces work separately.
- To help form the body, buy PVC pipes and make a rectangular shape. Then attach the body by creating ties to go over the PVC pipes. This also gives the students something to grip.
- A fine feature to add is dragon wings. Take a plain wooden dowel and wrap it around a paper wing cut-out. Attach them together. Paint designs to create a unique look. Have students operate the wings as an addition to the body. An example of a wing is below.
- Other options include purchasing a Chinese Dragon or having the students wear masks and connecting them with jump ropes.

Dragon Head

Dragon Wing

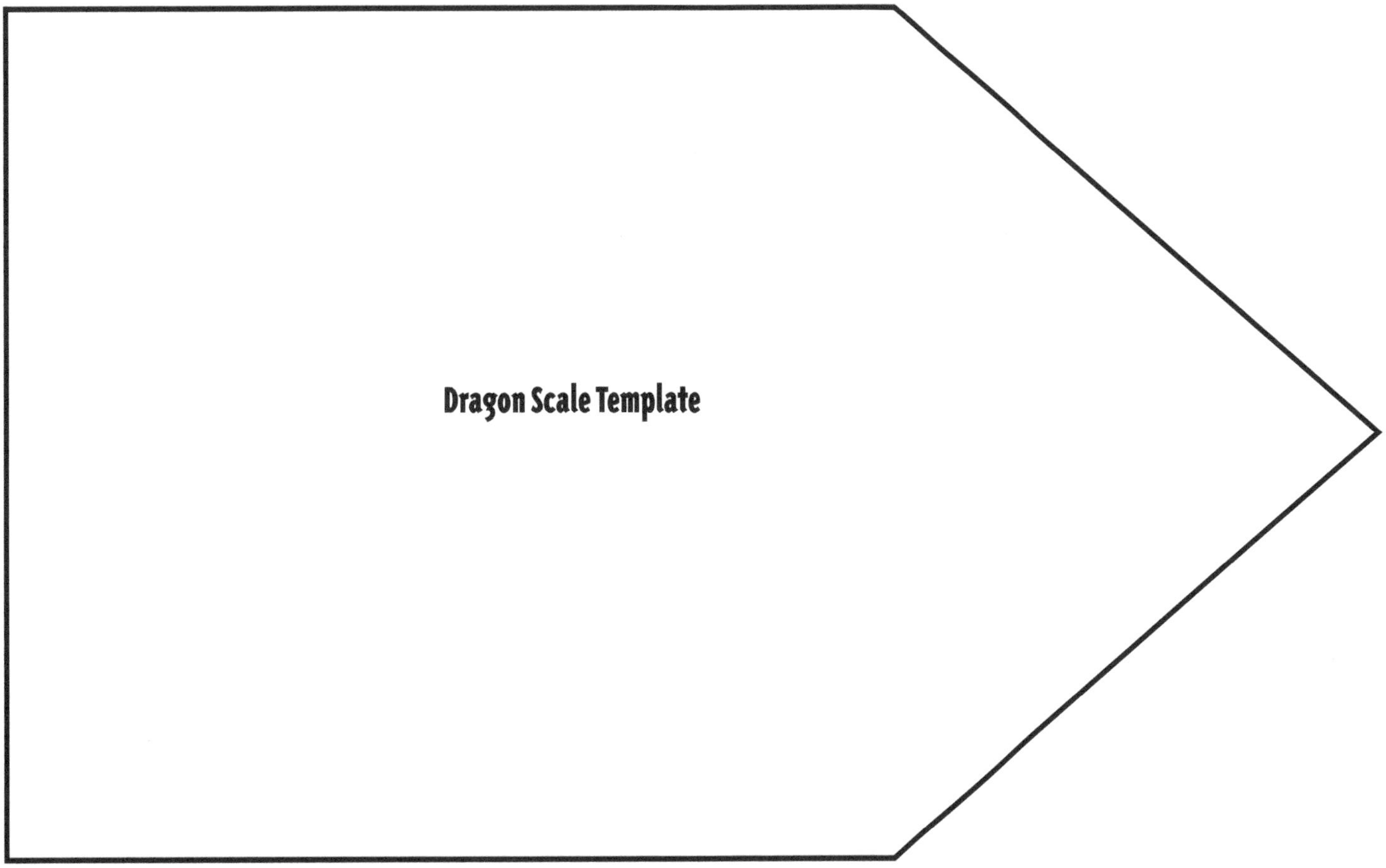

Dragon Dance

Introduction

RS	LS	RS/LS	RS/Jump
Macro	Macro	Micro	Micro

A Section

Sway R/L	Sway R/L	Tip-Toe Quick Step R/L/R/L	Sway R/L	Tip-Toe Quick Step R/L/R/L	Tip-Toe Quick Step R/L/R/L	Sway R/L	Body Circle Right	Body Circle Left
Macro	Macro	Micro	Macro	Micro	Micro	Macro	Whole Measure	Whole Measure

B Section (Repeat)

Gallop/Gallop/ Gallop/Hop	Gallop/Gallop/ Gallop/Hop	Gallop/Gallop/ Gallop/Hop	Gallop/Gallop/ Gallop/Hop	Body Circle Right (Circle Left 2nd Time)
Micro	Micro	Micro	Micro	Whole Measure

C Section (Repeat)

Up/Down/ Up/Down (Alternate with Partner)	Step R-R-L-L Step L-L-R-R (Alternate with Partner)	Up/Down/Up/Down (Alternate with Partner)	Step R-R-L-L Step L-L-R-R (Alternate with Partner)
Micro	Micro	Micro	Micro

B Section (Repeat)

A Section

Introduction

Dragon Speech Chant

Jennifer Kamradt

Dragon Dance

Jennifer Kamradt

A Section

B Section

C Section

Building Guy

Grade Level: 4–5

Concepts: Syncopation, Dynamics, Form, Bridge, Sixteenth Notes, and Thirds

Materials: SG/AG, SX/AX, SM/AM, BX, and CB

A Little History Behind the Piece:

On the way back from a school field trip, a teacher began confiscating from students a popular little children's toy used to build structures. Laughingly, she mentioned she was collecting "Building Guys." This thought stuck in her head, and thus the transition section was composed. The students now walk around the school singing "Building Guy."

Teaching Side Note:

The way each section builds upon each other and connects is similar to the content of this piece. Using the children's toy connection as an analogy is a great teaching tool when instructing about musical form.

Process

Suggested Form: A-Bridge-B-A-Bridge-C-D-Bridge/(Coda)

- Discuss the "leader." In this case, it will be the teacher until students are confident leading.
- Discuss what the leader will call out to move to the different sections. Each section is played as many times as necessary. The call could be "Building Guy" or simply "1-2-3-(Rest)."

A Section and Transition

- Introduce the A section. Play the rhythmic motive of A on a Tubano drum. Students can join in when they feel comfortable.
- Lead students to the observation of hand placement, and then the technique used. Ask students to write out the tones of the drum. B = Bass Tone, E = Edge
- Write in the rhythm above the notes. Have students practice playing the pattern of bass and edge tones using their hands on their legs.

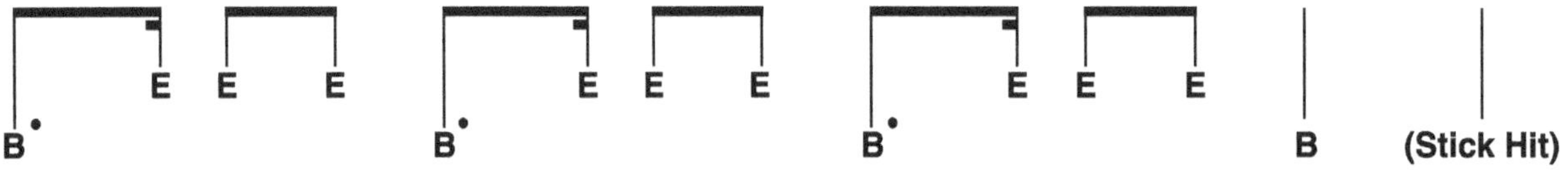

- Have students practice the pattern on drums. Transfer it to the barred instruments.
- Students can add a stick hit on the rest if desired.
- Discuss the different techniques on barred instruments and how to alternate the hands or use particular sticking for musical passages.
- Discuss that the bass tone = E and the edge tone = A.
- Introduce the transition or bridge. Give an overview of what a bridge does in music.
- Use "Building Guy" speech to teach rhythm. Practice by adding body percussion. Transfer the rhythm to the barred instruments.
- Really articulate the "Hey" at the end of the bridge.
- Practice going between the A section and the transition.

Note: At the end of the piece, the bridge actually turns into a coda. Discuss the difference between a bridge and a coda.

B Section

- Demonstrate the alto xylophone's syncopated rhythm and have all students join. Using speech to help review this rhythm from previous years can facilitate a fast learning process.
- Add a half note beat to the bass xylophone on low A.
- Add quarter note beats to stick hits for the soprano xylophone and alto metallophone. Discuss how to hit the sticks appropriately.
- Add the syncopated rhythm in the alto xylophone. After students become comfortable, add the soprano glockenspiel and alto glockenspiel line.
- Non-pitched percussion parts can easily be improvised with the barred instruments.
    - Shakers can play continuous eighth notes.
    - Cowbell or Agogo bell can play the beat.
    - Guiros can complement syncopated rhythms.
- Practice the B section and the transitions between the various sections.

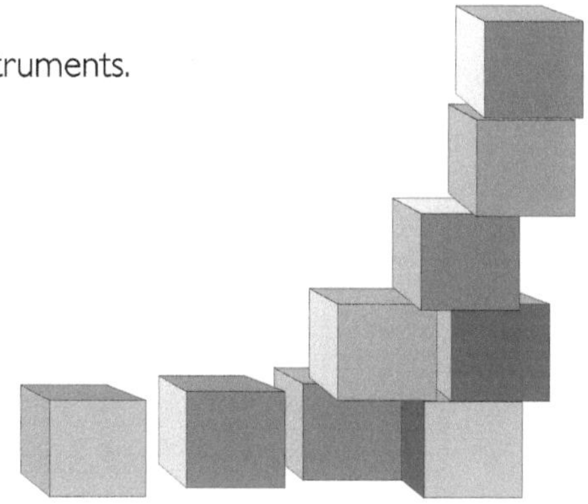

C and D Sections

- Teach the soprano glockenspiel and alto glockenspiel line to the students.
- Add the bass xylophone part as well as all the other barred instruments: alto metallophone, alto xylophone, and soprano xylophone.
- Practice until students become comfortable.
- Teach students on the cue to go straight to the D section and play eighth notes on "their" A.
    - Soprano glockenspiel, alto glockenspiel, and soprano xylophone are A above the staff.
    - Alto xylophone, soprano metallophone, alto metallophone, and bass xylophone are A in the staff.
- After sufficient time, bring the dynamics down to a *pianissimo* and end with a tremolo on "their" A.
- Work with students to develop dynamics through the whole piece.

Useful Tips

- This piece is great for developing a group dynamic. The arrangement works on playing together as an ensemble, and it establishes success quickly, easily, and with lots of fun!
- Remember to establish rules and clear boundaries with the barred instruments that must be followed to maintain classroom management.
- The use of speech will help with the syncopated rhythms. Saying "Syn-co-pa" is an effective tool for teaching the eighth-quarter-eighth note rhythm.
- Using a visual reference with form letters on a board helps to know which sections will be transitioned to next.
- To start the piece or to transition back to the A section, provide a melody or four-beat tone to signal the return.
- The process of this piece and rhythms can easily be turned into a drum circle exercise.

Building Guy

Jennifer Kamradt